FRENCH BREAD BAKING
FOR KIDS

Learn Delightful Recipes That Will Fill Your Home with an Attractive Smell of Freshly Baked French Bread

GoldInk Books

© **Copyright 2021 by GoldInk Books- All rights reserved.**

This document is geared towards providing exact and reliable information in regards to the topic and issue covered. The publication is sold with the idea that the publisher is not required to render accounting, officially permitted, or otherwise, qualified services. If advice is necessary, legal or professional, a practiced individual in the profession should be ordered.

- From a Declaration of Principles which was accepted and approved equally by a Committee of the American Bar Association and a Committee of Publishers and Associations.

It is not legal in any way to reproduce, duplicate, or transmit any part of this document in either electronic means or in printed format. Recording of this publication is strictly prohibited and any storage of this document is not allowed unless with written permission from the publisher. All rights reserved.

The information provided herein is stated to be truthful and consistent, in that any liability, in terms of inattention or otherwise, by any usage or abuse of any policies, processes, or directions contained within is the solitary and utter responsibility of the recipient reader. Under no circumstances will any legal responsibility or blame be held against the publisher for any reparation, damages, or monetary loss due to the information herein, either directly or indirectly.

Respective authors own all copyrights not held by the publisher.

The information herein is offered for informational purposes solely, and is universal as so. The presentation of the information is without contract or any type of guarantee assurance.

The trademarks that are used are without any consent, and the publication of the trademark is without permission or backing by the trademark owner. All trademarks and brands within this book are for clarifying purposes only and are the owned by the owners themselves, not affiliated with this document.

Contents

INTRODUCTION 7

CHAPTER 1: FRENCH BREAD BAKING AT A GLANCE 9

1.1 Bread Baking at Home 10

CHAPTER 2: BREAD BAKING PROBLEMS AND SOLUTIONS 12

CHAPTER 3: EASY AND QUICK BREAD BAKING RECIPES 14

3.1 Homemade Bakery French Bread 14

3.2 Four-Ingredient White Bread 16

3.3 Quick Pumpkin Bread 18

3.4 Banana Bread 20

3.5 Easy Tomato and Basil Bruschetta Bread 22

3.6 Apple Butter Bread 24

3.7 Soft Garlic Sticks 26

3.8 Olive Oil Bread 28

3.9 Easy Ciabatta Bread 29

3.10 Milk and Honey Bread 30

3.11 Sweet Potato Rolls Bread 31

3.12 Soft Pretzels 33

3.13 Peanut Butter Bread 35

3.14 Crusty Tea Bread 36

CHAPTER 4: FAMOUS FRENCH BREAD RECIPES 38

4.1 French Rye 38

4.2 Bread Machine Bagels 40

4.3 Chewy French Bread 42

4.4 Rosemary Bread 44

4.5 French Challah 46

4.6 French Flour Tortillas 47

4.7 French Pizza Dough 49

4.8 Light Sourdough Bread 50

4.9 Hamburger or Hot Dog Buns 52

4.10 Cracked Wheat Berry Bread 54

4.11 Apple Pie Cinnamon Rolls 56

4.12 French Donuts 58

4.13 Parmesan Garlic Bread 59

4.14 Chocolate Chip Brioche 60

CHAPTER 5: PARTICULAR INGREDIENTS FRENCH BREAD RECIPES 62

5.1 Rosemary Bread with Pecans and Dried Cranberries 62

5.2 Mushroom Bread 64

5.3 Black Pepper Focaccia Bread 66

5.4 Kalamata Olives Bread 68

5.5 Dill Pickle Rye Bread 69

5.6 Quinoa Oatmeal Bread 71

5.7 Banana Chocolate Chip Bread 73

5.8 Cinnamon Raisin Bread 75

5.9 Sweet French Bread 77

5.10 Chocolate Bread Recipe 78

5.11 Sweetened Condensed Milk White Bread 80

5.12 Potato Dinner Rolls with Honey Glaze 81

5.13 French Bear Claws 83

5.14 Golden Egg Bread with Dried Fruit 85

CHAPTER 6: DIET FRENCH BREAD RECIPES 86

6.1 Keto Bread 86

6.2 No-Milk Bread Recipe 88

6.3 Low Carb Yeast Bread 89

6.4 Fat-Free Wheat Bread 91

6.5 Whole-Wheat Bread 92

6.6 Oatmeal Bread Recipe 93

6.7 Basic White Bread (no-milk) 95

6.8 Gluten-Free Bread 96

6.9 Vegan Bread 98

6.10 Keto Sandwich Bread 99

6.11 Bread Maker Feta and Olive Crusty Low Carb Bread 101

6.12 Sugar-Free Bread 103

6.13 Gluten-Free Pizza Dough Recipe 104

CONCLUSION 106

Introduction

Do you like the aroma of fresh-baked bread in the morning?

If you answered yes to the question, it is time to start baking your bread!

Bread is one of the most widely consumed foods on the planet. The majority of dietary staples throughout the world are low-cost, high-energy plant-based foods. Although there are over 50,000 edible crops on the planet, just fifteen of them supply 90 percent of the world's food energy. Two-thirds of this is made up of rice, maize, and grain. The bread offers easy-to-digest carbs and minerals. It is a necessary food source that may also be enhanced to create a great output.

Bread is a nutrient-dense heritage from our forefathers, and anybody with a few tools and a basic understanding of dough can create a delicious loaf at home. Once you have made your first great bread at home, you will be hooked on bread-making. It is entertaining, tasty, and nutritious, and you can let off heat in the kitchen; it is a wonderful method to relieve stress.

Even though many people prefer freshly made bread, most of them continue to purchase packaged and often unhealthy baked goods from supermarkets. However, this is not needed! With only a few ingredients, you will be amazed at how fast you can create your bread.

This book is a must-have for every bread baker's bookshelf, whether professionals or home cooks. This attractive bread-making book includes step-by-step recipes and guidance, as well as a delicious selection of recipes for no-knead, kneaded, and enhanced bread. You will discover must-have techniques for resolving bread baking problems, as well as vital information about everything from preparation and proof periods to key vocabulary and kitchen necessities.

This bread cookbook will teach you how to master the art of bread baking so you can share your handmade loaves with those you care about. "Bread Baking for Kids" is the perfect bread guidebook for beginner bakers, providing clear instructions. This cookbook is also suggested for readers who wish to reduce weight and burn fat.

So, what exactly are you waiting for? Discover the many facets of baking and rediscover the joy of doing something nice for yourself and your flavor sensations. Make your favorite bread from home!

Chapter 1: French Bread Baking at a Glance

Bread is a very basic meal that has been consumed for thousands of years.

Ancient Egyptians have discovered it, British farmers collectively bringing dough to the local pie shop, and the cause of a reformation of France. Bread is a necessary yet tasty meal that is widely consumed. Only a few ingredients are required to create bread: flour, moisture, salt, and yeast. They form a structure when they mix, which is generated from the gluten in the wheat. The yeast generates important organic compounds and carbon dioxide gas as the gluten pattern develops.

The fermenting of the dough is induced by kneading, time, and heat. During the dough fermentation, a stronger gluten structure and taste are produced.

After the dough has developed enough, it is formed, proofed, and cooked in the oven after it has risen sufficiently.

The long, flat crusty baguette known as the "French sticks" is probably one of the most well-known symbols of French living. It is called a "baguette" in France, which translates to "a stick," and is the most famous bread in France, particularly in urban areas. The basic baguette weighs 200 grams (approximately half a pound); it found in three slightly various forms: the ordinary baguette, with its crunchy shining crust; the "shaped baguette", which is often a loaf produced by a factory bread-oven, and a lightly oiled baguette, or simple baguette. The three kinds of baguettes from anyone bakery will be fairly similar.

1.1 Bread Baking at Home

The bread baker aims to transform wheat starch into a delicious, multilayered bread while knowing how to control time and

temperature during the breadmaking process.

The baker's hands, eyes, hearing, taste, senses, artistic touches, and experience all play a part in the recipe's ultimate success.

Making bread at home was formerly thought to be a talent that all bakers had. It is not as popular these days, but getting started has never been simpler. Making delicious bread for yourself and your family is a gratifying and healthful pastime. It is also something you are always learning. There is no such thing as too much

information, and even seasoned professional bakers continue to learn daily.

Kneading the bread until it produces gluten is required for regular bread baking. The major difference between the wet dough method and the dry dough method is kneading.

A simpler kind of bread may be made in less time and does not need overnight proofing. As a gas-filled ball, most beginning bakers are frightened to handle their bread dough after it first rises. If you divide your bread dough several times before shaping it, the gluten becomes stronger, and the dough does not deflate. A crisper crust may be achieved by scoring your soured dough with a paring blade. There is just one guideline for scoring bread: do not cut too deeply, but leave marks. This allows the bread to open up and grow while it bakes. You may also score the bread with sharp scissors or pointed razors. On a baguette loaf, bakers typically cut four lines parallel to the long edge of the loaf.

To produce gluten during kneading, bread flour must be rich in protein. This allows the bread to rise throughout the fermenting process. Bread flour is a high-protein flour that is sold by most manufacturers and is excellent for baking bread at home.

If you want to be healthier, use whole wheat flour instead of 1/3 of the white wheat flour in your preparations. It may take from twenty to thirty minutes to bake a loaf of bread. Ordinarily, white bread is cooked for 25 minutes, while fuller bread may take 40 to 45 minutes to bake. It all depends on the type you are preparing. If you are baking a moist dough with several ingredients, the baking time will be longer owing to the low oven temperature.

Chapter 2: Bread Baking Problems and Solutions

There are many problems that a bread baker can face while preparing bread for the first time. The common problems and their solutions are described in this chapter.

During the baking process, the bread cracked.

When you bake bread, it grows, but you want to keep that expansion under control.

Cutting the bread horizontally or diagonally across the surface encourages it to develop in a certain direction.

When I cut prepared bread, it crumbles and comes apart

People frequently do this if the batter is too thick, and they add additional flour instead of kneading through it, resulting in crumbly bread.

During baking, the bread rises unevenly.

Place it on the baking pan and let it proof for 40 minutes; the air pressure you have generated will result in the ideal cob.

My fingers and the worktop are both clinging to the dough.

The answer is dependent on the kind of bread you are baking. To give the loaf air pockets, items like focaccia have a fluid dough. The dough is usually moist and sticky at first, but after four to seven minutes of kneading, it gets less slippery and glossier as skin forms, which is the gluten-producing process. You will eventually reach a stage when the dough is no longer sticky, and your hands have become clean just by kneading. Give it another sprinkling of flour if it appears to be taking too long.

The final loaf is thick and mushy.

Always form your loaf on a sheet of nonstick parchment paper, then place it directly on the hot rock and lower the oven temperature to approximately 180-200°C after it has proven. The bottoms of most loaves are mushy because they have not been heated, but you can get a similar effect at home by using a hot rock.

Boosting dough's rise

Many contemporary ovens may be adjusted to a very low temperature, allowing you to prove your bread in 30-40 minutes. Put the dough in a chilly oven and turn on the light; the heat from the lamp will help it rise. You may also consider adding a spoon of sugar to provide more food for the yeast.

The dough is not rising at all.

Many people believe that dough will not rise unless they leave it out for many hours and in a very warm environment. To make the dough rise, you should not need anything extra. You do not need to put it somewhere warm; just set it on the side, and it will grow in one or two hours. It may be the yeast if that does not raise - new yeast can be problematic. It may also destroy the yeast if you use boiled water or add acidic substances or specific spices.

Chapter 3: Easy and Quick Bread Baking Recipes

3.1 Homemade Bakery French Bread

Children can even make this bread. It is that simple. Kneading dough at home is a difficult job, and it is easy to get overwhelmed by the procedure. This Homemade French Bread takes a little over an hour to make, so you can enjoy delicious, fresh bread when the kids got home from school.

Cooking Time: 1 hour 5 minutes

Serving Size: 8 servings

Ingredients:

- 6 ½ cups flour
- 1 egg for brushing on bread
- 2 ½ teaspoons salt
- 1/3 cup oil
- 2 tablespoons yeast
- 2 cups hot water
- 3 tablespoons sugar
- ½ cup warm water

Method:

1. Dissolve the yeast in ½ cup hot water in a small dish.
2. Stir together boiled water, salt, oil, sweetener, and three cups of flour in a large mixing dish.
3. Fill a dish halfway with the yeast mixture.
4. One cup at a time, add the rest 3 and a half cups of flour.
5. Divide the dough into three equal halves.
6. Form into a loaf of French bread and trim the edges.

7. Make 3-4 diagonal slices in the bread using a blade.
8. Brush with a beaten egg.
9. Allow dough to rise for 45 minutes in a hot place.
10. Preheat oven to 375°F and bake for 18-24 minutes, or until lightly browned.

3.2 Four-Ingredient White Bread

When you are stuck at the house, this is the ideal simple bread recipe to prepare. There are just four ingredients and less than ten minutes of hands-on time required. The only way to simplify it is to use a regular loaf pan rather than a round dish with high edges. You just need flour, yeast, seasoning, and liquid to get started. This method does not even need mixing, so there's no need for a machine.

Cooking Time: 8 hours 55 minutes

Serving Size: 16 slices

Ingredients:

- ½ teaspoon active dry yeast
- 1 teaspoon salt
- 1.5 cups warm water
- 3 cups all-purpose flour

Method:

1. Combine all four ingredients in a large mixing dish.
2. Cover dish with cling film and set aside to rest for 8 to 20 hours at room temperature.
3. Flour a work surface thoroughly.
4. Take the dough out of the dish with a spatula and gently put it onto the work surface.
5. Take the upper and bottom corners of the dough with floured hands and squeeze them together in the center to create a loaf form.
6. Heat the oven to 425°F and set aside the dough for thirty minutes to rest.
7. Make a long cut across the surface of the dough with a sharp knife.

8. Bake for 50-60 minutes, or until golden brown on top.
9. Remove the bread from the pan and set it aside to cool for at least 15-20 minutes before cutting with a sharp blade.

3.3 Quick Pumpkin Bread

Easy Pumpkin Loaf offers a basic pumpkin flavor and is a no-fail fast bread. This Pumpkin Bread is ideal for brunch or a meal at any time of the day. This simple pumpkin bread recipe yields two loaves: one to enjoy and one to give away. When kept in the freezer, pumpkin bread lasts approximately a week.

Cooking Time: 1 hour

Serving Size: 20 slices

Ingredients:

- 2 teaspoons cinnamon
- 2 teaspoons pumpkin pie spice
- 1 teaspoon baking soda
- 2 teaspoons baking powder
- 385 grams all-purpose flour
- 1 teaspoon salt
- 2 teaspoons vanilla extract
- 2 cups solid pack pumpkin
- 435 grams granulated sugar
- 3 large eggs
- 1 cup coconut oil

Method:

1. Combine the oil, vanilla, eggs, sweetener, and pumpkins in a medium-sized mixing bowl.
2. Combine the flour, baking powder, salts, pumpkin pie spice, baking soda, cinnamon in a small dish.
3. Combine the wet and dry items in a mixing bowl and stir just until mixed. Do not overmix the ingredients.

4. Grease and flour 2 9-inch loaf pans.
5. Divide the mixture into two plates
6. Preheat oven to 325°F and bake for 45-50 minutes, or until a wooden skewer in the middle comes out clean.

3.4 Banana Bread

Banana bread is fluffy and tasty bread. It is simple to prepare, and there's no need for a blender! Ripe bananas, eggs, baking powder, bread, vanilla extract, sugar, and flour. For almost a decade, this banana bread is the most requested recipe. Everything may be mixed in one dish, and the quantity of sugar or bananas can be changed.

Cooking Time: 65 minutes

Serving Size: 1 loaf (8-10 servings)

Ingredients:

- 1 teaspoon vanilla extract
- 1 ½ cups all-purpose flour
- 3/4 cup sugar
- 1 large egg
- 3 medium very ripe bananas
- ½ teaspoon baking soda
- 1 pinch salt
- 1/3 cup butter

Method:

1. Preheat oven to 325 degrees Fahrenheit and grease a 4x8-inch loaf dish.
2. Smash the ripe bananas with a knife in a mixing dish until totally smooth.
3. In a mixing bowl, combine the mashed bananas and the softened butter.
4. Combine the baking soda and salts in a mixing bowl.
5. Combine the sweetener, egg mixture, and vanilla essence in a mixing bowl.

6. Add the flour and stir to combine.
7. Pour the mixture into the loaf pan that has been prepared.
8. Preheat the oven to 350°F (175°C) and bake for 50 to 60 minutes, or until a tester or bamboo skewer inserted in the middle comes out clean.
9. Turn off the heat and set it aside to cool for a few moments in the pan.
10. Cut into slices and serve.

3.5 Easy Tomato and Basil Bruschetta Bread

This traditional appetizer, called "bruschetta," is a great way to combine the tastes of farm-fresh tomatoes, fresh herbs, clove, and olive oil. Because you can prepare a large quantity of the toppings ahead of time and toast the baguette pieces, it is ideal for a party.

Cooking Time: 35 minutes

Serving Size: 6-10 servings

Ingredients:

- 1 baguette
- ¼ cup olive oil
- ¾ teaspoon sea salt
- ½ teaspoon black pepper
- 1 teaspoon balsamic vinegar
- 8 fresh sliced basil leaves
- 7 ripe tomatoes
- 1 tablespoon extra-virgin olive oil
- 2 cloves garlic

Method:

1. Bring 2 quarts of water to a boil.
2. Remove the saucepan from the heat after the water has reached a boil.
3. Blanch the vegetables for 30 seconds in boiling water.
4. Preheat the oven to 425°F (230°C) and place a rack in the highest position.
5. Toss tomatoes with clove, basil, vinegar, sunflower oil, salt, and pepper in a mixing bowl.

6. Combine the extra-virgin olive oil, garlic, and balsamic vinegar in a mixing bowl.
7. Slice the bread on the side using a bread knife to make half-inch thick pieces.
8. Drizzle one side of each piece with olive oil and put on a cooking sheet or roasting pan with the olive oil side downwards.
9. Toast the pieces for four to six minutes on the top shelf of the oven until gently browned all around sides.

3.6 Apple Butter Bread

This bread has a rich taste and stays moist for many days after baking, thanks to the apple butter. The mixture, which can be prepared with only one pan and a whisk, has a touch of heartiness due to the whole-wheat flour.

Cooking Time: 1 hour

Serving Size: 8 servings

> **Ingredients:**
> - 60 milliliters plain yogurt
> - Turbinado sugar
> - 1 ½ teaspoons vanilla extract
> - 180 milliliters apple butter
> - 110 grams dark brown sugar
> - 2 large eggs
> - 120 milliliters vegetable oil
> - 100 grams granulated sugar
> - ¼ teaspoon nutmeg
> - ½ teaspoon fine sea salt
> - 130 grams all-purpose flour
> - 1 teaspoon ground cinnamon
> - ½ teaspoon ground allspice
> - 1 teaspoon baking soda
> - 60 grams whole-wheat flour

Method:

1. Preheat the oven to 350°F and coat a 9-by-5-inch bread pan generously with cooking spray.
2. Toss together the baking soda, whole-wheat flour, all-purpose flour, allspice, nutmeg, cinnamon, and salt in a large mixing bowl.
3. Whisk together the oil, honey, and brown sugar in a large mixing dish.
4. Add the eggs one at a time, whisking well after each inclusion to ensure well incorporated.
5. In a separate bowl, whisk together the vanilla essence and the sugar.
6. Stir in the dry ingredients until it is completely combined.
7. Combine the apple butter and yogurt in a mixing bowl and stir well to combine.
8. Spread the batter evenly in the loaf pan that has been prepared.
9. Using a large amount of turbinado sugar, cover the whole surface of the bread.
10. Bake for 35 to 40 minutes, or until a toothpick inserted in the middle comes out clean.

3.7 Soft Garlic Sticks

These smooth, buttery breadsticks do not disappoint with their aroma and pleasant crunch. They are very tasty and go well with soups, sauces, salads, and any other dish that calls with something heavy on the side. Make a batch of these delectable breadsticks to go with your next dinner.

Cooking Time: 55 minutes

Serving Size: 1 loaf

Ingredients:

For the Dough

- 1 ¾ teaspoon kosher salt
- 3 cups bread flour
- 2 tablespoons granulated sugar
- 3 tablespoons butter melted
- 1 ½ teaspoon instant yeast
- 1 cup warm water

For Brushing

- ¼ teaspoon garlic powder
- ¼ teaspoon Italian seasoning
- ½ teaspoon kosher salt
- 3 tablespoons butter melted

Method:

1. Mix all dough components, except flour, in the dish of an electrical stick blender equipped with the dough hook.
2. Continue adding flour at medium speed.
3. Increase the speed to high and mix for 7 minutes, or until the dough is thick and flexible.
4. Make 12 pieces out of the dough.

5. Each portion of dough should be rolled into a 7-inch log.
6. For 1 hour, place bread logs on a nonstick baking surface.
7. Preheat oven to 350°F and bake for 12 minutes, until it's lightly browned.
8. In a small bowl, mix the salt, butter, and garlic.
9. Remove the breadsticks from the oven and brush them with the butter mixture right away.

3.8 Olive Oil Bread

This basic olive oil bread is quick and easy to prepare, and it does not even need fermentation! Fresh bread can be on the table in moments!

Cooking Time: 15 minutes

Serving Size: 2 loaves

Ingredients:

- ½ teaspoon salt
- 1/3 cup warm water
- 1 teaspoon baking powder
- 2 tablespoon olive oil
- 1 cup all-purpose flour

Method:

1. Mix the baking powder, flour, and salt in a large mixing bowl.
2. Mix in the coconut oil and water until well combined.
3. Heat a big cast iron or nonstick pan on the stove until it is hot.
4. To gently coat the pan, drizzle it with butter and swirl it around.
5. Make four tiny patties out of the dough.
6. Cook for five minutes on each side in a preheated saucepan over medium heat.

3.9 Easy Ciabatta Bread

The leftover ciabatta bread could be used for lunch; it makes excellent French toast. It is nutrient-dense and can be made using basic ingredients.

Cooking Time: 50 minutes

Serving Size: 4 servings

Ingredients:

- 8 (1-ounce) slices of ciabatta bread
- 2 tablespoons butter
- ½ teaspoon ground cinnamon
- 2 large eggs
- ⅓ cup fresh orange juice
- ½ cup 2% reduced-fat milk
- ½ cup orange marmalade/jam

Method:

1. In a medium saucepan over a moderate flame, combine the juice and jam; bring to a boil.
2. Remove from the heat and set aside to keep warm.
3. In a small bowl, mix together the cinnamon, milk, and yolks.
4. Dip bread pieces two or three times in the egg mixture and set aside for 20 seconds each time.
5. In a large nonstick pan, melt 1 tablespoon oil over moderate flame.
6. Cook for 2 minutes a side or until gently browned in a pan. Drizzle marmalade syrup over the top.

3.10 Milk and Honey Bread

This bread symbolizes the wheat-growing area because of its ingredients. This bread does not last longer than a week at home. It is really simple to create.

Cooking Time: 30 minutes

Serving Size: 2 loaves (16 slices each)

Ingredients:

- 2 teaspoons salt
- 8 cups all-purpose flour
- 1/3 cup honey
- ¼ cup butter
- 2-½ cups warm whole milk
- 2 packages of active dry yeast

Method:

1. Put yeast in hot milk in a large mixing bowl.
2. Combine salt, oil, honey, and 5 cups flour in a mixing bowl and whisk until smooth.
3. To make a smooth paste, add leftover flour.
4. Turn out onto a dusted board and knead for 6-10 minutes, or until thick and flexible.
5. Place in an oiled mixing bowl and turn to grease the top.
6. Punch down the dough and divide it into two loaves.
7. Allow 30 minutes for the dough to double in size.
8. Preheat oven to 375°F and bake for 30-40 minutes, or until lightly browned.

3.11 Sweet Potato Rolls Bread

Sweet Potato Meal Rolls have a light and cuddly texture with a little crunchy and sticky crust and a touch of sweet potato flavor.

Cooking Time: 55 minutes

Serving Size: 15 rolls

Ingredients:

For the Dough

- 1 ½ teaspoon fine salt
- 4 ¾ cups bread flour
- 2 tablespoons honey
- 2 ¼ teaspoons instant yeast
- 4 tablespoons melted butter
- 2 whole eggs
- 1 cup (240 ml) whole milk
- 250 grams sweet potato

For Baking

- Coarse salt
- 1 large egg

Method:

1. Add the buttermilk, yeast, eggs, honey, butter, and sweet potato to the mixing bowl.
2. Stir in the salt and 2 cups flour with a metal spoon till the dough resembles a rough, stiff lump.
3. Connect the dough hooks to the machine, reduce the speed to moderate, and gradually add half flour, mixing until a dough mass develops.

4. Place the dough in a big clean bowl that has been lightly sprayed with cooking spray.
5. Allow it to rise at ambient temperature for 45-50 minutes to 1 hour, or until the mixture is puffy and approximately doubled in size.
6. Dampen the dough slightly.
7. Cut the dough into fifteen equal pieces using a bench scraper, fork, or tortilla wheel.
8. Form each portion into a ball and put it in the pan that has been prepared.
9. Preheat the oven to 350°F and bake the rolls for 20 to 30 minutes, or until lightly browned.

3.12 Soft Pretzels

The soft pretzel batter is a family recipe and requires just 10 to 15 minutes to rest before molding. The pretzels get their characteristic taste from baking soda boiling. You just need the fewest, most simple items, and you already have them in your kitchen.

Cooking Time: 40 minutes

Serving Size: 12 pretzels

Ingredients:

- 4 cups all-purpose flour
- Coarse sea salt for sprinkling
- 1 tablespoon brown sugar
- 1 tablespoon unsalted butter
- 1 packet active dry
- 1 teaspoon salt
- 1½ cups warm water

Baking Soda Bath

- 9 cups water
- ½ cup baking soda

Method:

1. In a bowl of warm water, dissolve the yeast.
2. Allow 1 minute for the mixture to settle.
3. Combine the brown sugar, salt, and softened butter in a mixing bowl.
4. Gradually add 3 cups of flour, one cup at a time.
5. Stir with a metal spoon until a firm dough forms.

6. Add another ¾ cup of flour until the mixture no longer sticks together.
7. Preheat the oven to 400 degrees Fahrenheit.
8. Split the dough into 1/3 cup pieces using a scalpel blade or pizza cutter.
9. Make a 20-inch rope out of the dough.
10. Bring the two sides of the dough together at the bottom of the circular to form around. Twist the ends of the rope together.
11. In a large saucepan, bring baking powder and 9 cups water to a simmer.
12. For 20-30 seconds, drop 1-2 pretzels into hot water.
13. Place the pretzel on the baking sheet. Sprinkle with salt.
14. Preheat oven to 350°F and bake for 12-15 minutes, or until lightly browned.

3.13 Peanut Butter Bread

The Peanut Butter Loaf recipe comes out fantastically when prepared. It is the ideal morning bread, lightly toasted and covered with jelly. You should certainly give it a try as soon as possible.

Cooking Time: 1 hour

Serving Size: 12 servings

Ingredients:

- 1 tablespoon baking powder
- 1 ¾ cups all-purpose flour
- 1 cup peanut butter
- 1 teaspoon kosher salt
- 2 large eggs
- 2/3 cup granulated sugar
- 1 cup fat-free milk

Method:

1. Preheat the oven to 350 degrees Fahrenheit.
2. In a blender jar, combine the milk, honey, yolks, and peanut butter.
3. Secure the cover and mix until completely smooth.
4. Close the cover and add the remaining items.
5. Blend a few times to combine the flour.
6. Fill a greased 9-x-5-inch loaf pan halfway with batter.
7. Preheat oven to 350°F and bake for half an hour, or until a sharp toothpick inserted in the center comes out clean.

3.14 Crusty Tea Bread

According to the ingredients, this dish is soy-free, plant-based, dairy-free, peanut-free, egg-free, and vegetarian. Place the materials in the order given in your bread maker according to the manufacturers' instructions and cook on the European bread cycle to create this bread.

Cooking Time: 3 hours 5 minutes

Serving Size: 1 small loaf (about 1 pound)

Ingredients:

- 1 teaspoon salt
- 1½ teaspoons active dry yeast
- 2 cups all-purpose
- ¾ cup extra-strong black tea

Method:

1. In a stand mixer, pour the cooled tea.
2. Allow 5 minutes for the yeast to ferment.
3. Stir in part of the flour and the spices until everything is well combined.
4. Make the dough for 10 minutes after adding the additional flour.
5. Cover and set aside for 1 hour in a hot place. Punch down the dough.
6. Place the dough in the prepared pan and form it into a loaf.
7. Allow rising for approximately 1 hour, or until doubled in size.
8. Bake for 15 to 30 minutes at 350°F, or until golden brown, crispy, and hollow when tapped.

9. Allow the loaf to rest for 5 minutes before transferring it to a wire rack to finish cooling.

Chapter 4: Famous French Bread Recipes

4.1 French Rye

This tasty European-style rye receives a taste boost from cider in the dough, which Saveur magazine named one of the finest breads in the country. Offer it sliced with Dijon, cheese, or paté for warm or cold toast.

Cooking Time:

Serving Size:

Ingredients:

For the Starter

- 2/3 cup water
- 1 cup bread flour
- 2 teaspoon dry yeast

For the Dough

- 2 teaspoon salt
- 1 cup water
- 3 cups rye flour
- ½ cup bread flour

Method:

1. In a mixing dish, dissolve the yeast in the liquid.
2. Allow sitting for 5 minutes before stirring to dissolve.
3. Mix in the flour to make a thick batter.
4. In a large mixing bowl, combine the flour and salt.
5. Create a well in the middle and pour in a quarter of the water and the starters.
6. In the center, stir in the flour.

7. To get a very wet, sticky dough, mix in the excess liquid.
8. Knead the dough for approximately 10 minutes on a floured surface until silky and flexible.
9. Form the dough into two long loaves by dividing it into two equal sections.
10. Preheat the oven to 200 degrees Celsius.
11. Bake for 45 minutes, or until soft when touched on the bottom.
12. Allow cooling on a cutting board.

4.2 Bread Machine Bagels

This simple homemade bagel recipe demonstrates that you can create wonderfully chewy bagels in your own house with only a few simple ingredients and baking equipment! Bagels are simpler to shape than they seem.

Cooking Time: 3 hours

Serving Size: 8 Bagels

Ingredients:

- 2 teaspoons olive oil
- 1 egg white beaten
- 1 tablespoon granulated sugar
- 2 teaspoons salt
- 2-¾ teaspoons instant dry yeast
- 4 cups bread flour
- 1½ cups warm water

For Boiling

- ¼ cup honey
- 2 quarts water

Method:

1. In the pan of your bread machine equipped with a dough hook function, whisk together the hot water and yeast.
2. Let for 5 minutes of resting time after covering.
3. Combine the brown sugar, flour, and salt in a mixing bowl.
4. For 2 - 3 minutes, beat on moderate speed.
5. Using oil or nonstick spray, lightly oil a large mixing bowl.
6. Position the dough in the bowl and flip it to coat it with oil on both sides.
7. Cut the dough into eight pieces.

8. Preheat the oven to 425 degrees Fahrenheit.
9. Fill a big, broad saucepan halfway with water.
10. Add the honey and whisk to combine. Bring the mixture to a boil, then lower to a moderate heat setting.
11. Place 2-4 bagels in at a time, ensuring they have enough space to float. Cook for 1 minute or two of the bagels.
12. Place 4 bagels on each baking sheet.
13. Preheat the oven to 350°F and bake for 20-25 minutes, turning the pan midway through.

4.3 Chewy French Bread

Crispy French Bread is a five-ingredient bread that is quick and simple to make. It is delicious, dipped in soup, on a toast, or just eaten with a piece of butter! Instead of using a blender, you may certainly prepare this recipe by hand.

Cooking Time: 2 hours 25 minutes

Serving Size: 20 slices

Ingredients:

- 2 ½ cups warm water
- 6 cups all-purpose flour
- 1 tablespoon white sugar
- 2 teaspoons salt
- 1 tablespoon yeast

Method:

1. Mix the salt, sugar, yeast, and hot water in a large standing mixer.
2. Make sure you use hot water rather than boiling.
3. To get the yeast to activate, mix everything and let it rest for approximately 15 minutes.
4. Add 5-6 cups flour slowly until you get the desired consistency.
5. Add the dough to a large mixing bowl that has been greased with canola oil.
6. Form the dough into a smooth ball using your hands.
7. Make two big oblong forms out of the dough. Using a large oiled cookie sheet or a French bread pan, bake the bread.
8. Cover with a cloth and let it for another 30-40 minutes to rise.
9. Bake for half an hour at 400 degrees, or until the bottom is somewhat brown and crispy and the top is lightly browned.

10. Remove from oven and cool on a wire rack.

4.4 Rosemary Bread

This Easy Rosemary Loaf takes just five minutes to prepare, 10 minutes to form, and it sounds like it came straight from an excellent bakery. The recipe must require the least amount of work and time to prepare.

Cooking Time: 43 minutes

Serving Size: 18 slices

Ingredients:

- 1 tablespoon melted butter
- 1 teaspoon flaky sea salt
- 3 tablespoon rosemary
- 2 cups tap water
- 2 teaspoons kosher salt
- 1 teaspoon active dry yeast
- 4 cups bread flour

Method:

1. Mix the wheat yeast, salt, flour, and rosemary in a medium-large mixing bowl. Make a well in the middle and fill it with water.
2. Roll it up with cling film and set aside to rising night or for up to 16 hours at room temperature.
3. Preheat the oven to 425 degrees Fahrenheit.
4. On a worktop, spread a generous ¼ cup of flour.
5. Put the dough onto the lightly floured dish and flip it a few times to coat it.
6. Cut the dough into two or three pieces that are about equal in size.

7. Coarsely dice rosemary, and sea salt is gently sprinkled on top.
8. Place the pan in the oven. Bake for 23-28 minutes, or until lightly browned.
9. Place the bread on a cooling rack to finish cooling.

4.5 French Challah

Begin your day off right with this delicious challah French toast, gently scented with honey, cinnamon, and spice.

Cooking Time: 40 minutes

Serving Size: 4 Challah

Ingredients:

- 2 ½ tablespoons butter
- Four braided challahs
- ½ teaspoon pure vanilla extract
- Pinch of nutmeg
- 3 extra-large eggs
- ½ teaspoon cinnamon
- ½ cup milk

Method:

1. Combine the eggs, milk, cinnamon, vanilla, and nutmeg in a large shallow baking dish or container and whisk until well combined.
2. Dip 1 challah piece at a time in the beaten egg, flipping the bread many times.
3. Meantime, in a big heavy pan, heat the butter until it begins to bubble.
4. Cook for 2 minutes, or until 2 of the wet challah slices are nicely browned on the bottom.
5. Cook for another 2 minutes on the second side, or until lightly golden.

4.6 French Flour Tortillas

This is the ideal solution when you cannot purchase your favorite cake or just do not have time to create your multicolored crêpe cake. The chew will get softer and more delicate the longer the tortilla sits in the soak.

Cooking Time: 45 minutes

Serving Size: 8 tortillas

Ingredients:

For the French Toast

- 8 medium flour tortillas
- Butter, for pan
- Pinch ground nutmeg
- Pinch kosher salt
- 1 teaspoon pure vanilla extract
- ½ teaspoon ground cinnamon
- 2 tablespoon heavy cream
- 2 tablespoon packed brown sugar
- ¼ cup whole milk
- 2 large eggs

Method:

1. Whisk together the eggs, nutmeg, cream, sugar, milk, cinnamon, vanilla, and salt in a large mixing bowl until smooth.
2. Add the tortillas one at a time, turning them to ensure that they are well covered in the mixture.
3. Allow at least fifteen minutes, and up to thirty minutes, for all tortillas to marinate.

4. Melt a tiny tab of butter in a large pan over medium-low heat.
5. Cook one moistened tortilla in a pan until brown on both sides, about 2 minutes on each side.
6. If preferred, top with whipped cream and berries, then drizzle with chocolate sauce or dust with icing sugar.

4.7 French Pizza Dough

This dish is definitely worth the time and effort. It is "Homestyle Pizza Night" at your home when you add some sauces, cheese, and toppings!

Cooking Time: 35 minutes

Serving Size: 16 slices

Ingredients:

- Cornmeal
- Olive oil
- 9 cups flour
- 1 tablespoon salt
- 2 (¼ ounce) packages of dry yeast
- 1 tablespoon sugar
- 3 ½ cups lukewarm water

Method:

1. Add sugar in warm water and dissolve the yeast.
2. Add 4 cups flour and a pinch of salt.
3. With a wooden spoon, thoroughly combine all ingredients.
4. Add the remaining flour, one cup at a time.
5. Place the dough in an oil-coated mixing bowl.
6. Allow rising until it has doubled in size.
7. Allow for 15 minutes of resting time after cutting into two pieces.
8. Spread your preferred sauce, cheeses, and toppings on top.

4.8 Light Sourdough Bread

The Sourdough Starting course makes it simple to make sourdough bread. It is not as sour as classic sourdough bread, but it is still smooth and creamy like normal bread! It is best served with a dollop of creamy butter.

Cooking Time: 55 minutes

Serving Size: 1 loaf

> **Ingredients:**
>
> **Sourdough Starter**
>
> - 2 cups bread flour
> - 2 teaspoon active dry yeast
> - 1-½ cups water
>
> **Light Sourdough Bread**
>
> - 1-½ teaspoon salt
> - 2 teaspoon active dry yeast
> - 3 cups bread flour
> - 2 tablespoon sugar
> - 2 tablespoon lemon juice
> - 3 tablespoon apple cider vinegar

Method:

1. To make the sourdough starters, combine all of the ingredients in a mixing bowl.
2. Assemble the kneading wheels and place all of the "Sourdough Starter" items in the dish in the sequence indicated.
3. Close the lid and connect the power cable into the socket after placing the baking pan in the "Home Baker".
4. Press "Start" after selecting the "Sourdough Starter" level.

5. In the baking pan, combine all of the items for "Light Sourdough Bread" in the order given to the finished sourdough starter.
6. Press "Start" after setting the crust controller to the desired thickness.
7. Hold down the "Setup" or "Stop" button once the baking is finished.
8. Using protective gloves, remove the bread from the baking pan and shake it out thoroughly.

4.9 Hamburger or Hot Dog Buns

Hamburgers taste incredible when they are served on homemade bread. Make a batch of buns earlier this season and store them if you live in a region where the weather is so hot that you do not want to warm your oven.

Cooking Time: 2 hours 30 minutes

Serving Size: 18 buns

Ingredients:

- 6 cups all-purpose flour
- 1 egg beaten
- 2 tablespoons vegetable oil
- 2 teaspoons salt
- ½ cup warm water
- 2 cups warm milk
- 2 packets active dry yeast
- 2 tablespoons sugar

Method:

1. Mix the sugar and yeast in hot water in a large mixing dish.
2. To the yeast mixture, add oil, salt, milk, and 3 cups of flour. Beat for two minutes.
3. Add the flour ¼ cup at a time until the dough starts to pull away from the edges of the dish.
4. Place the dough in an oiled mixing bowl.
5. Place the dough on a lightly greased work surface and roll it out.
6. Divide the mixture into 18 equal portions.
7. Make a ball out of each component.

8. Flatten the spheres into 3 ½" discs for hamburger buns.
9. Preheat your oven to 400°F 15 minutes before you plan to bake the buns.
10. Bake for 20 minutes, just until the loaf reaches a core temperature of 190°F.

4.10 Cracked Wheat Berry Bread

It is white bread with crushed whole wheat berries that are nubby, crispy, and earthy. It is easy to prepare using a bread machine. Put wheat berries in this loaf and cook them. They provide incredible texture, taste, and nutrients to the recipe.

Cooking Time: 4 hours 30 minutes

Serving Size: 16 slices

Ingredients:

- 2 tablespoons unsalted butter
- 2 teaspoons instant yeast
- 1- ½ teaspoon table salt
- 1 teaspoon sugar
- ½ cup whole-grain wheat berries
- 1 cup warm milk
- 2- ½ cups bread flour

Method:

1. Boil the wheat berries for twenty minutes in 1 cup of water.
2. Add 1 cup bread flour and 1 cup prepared wheat berries in a spice grinder.
3. Using a food processor, finely chop the wheat berries.
4. Combine the butter, salt, milk, sugar, 180-gram leftover flour, the ground wheat berries and flour combination, and the yeast in a mixing bowl.
5. Start by selecting the dough cycle.
6. Pull the dough from the beginning to the end until it is smooth, then pinch closed each piece.
7. Preheat the oven to 425 degrees Fahrenheit.

8. Bake for 20-30 minutes, or until the internal temperature hits 190 degrees F and the bottom is golden and hollow, in a preheated oven.//

9. Allow bread for an hour to cool on the rack before slicing.

4.11 Apple Pie Cinnamon Rolls

These are the cinnamon buns you have always wanted—gooey in the middle and topped with cream cheese icing. When you add the tart apples, you have got yourself a real cinnamon roll.

Cooking Time: 1 hour

Serving Size: 12 rolls

Ingredients:

For the Dough

- 2 teaspoons salt
- 4 cups bread flour
- 1/3 cup melted butter
- 1 egg, room temperature
- 1 package yeast
- ½ cup granulated sugar
- ½ cup scalded milk
- ½ cup lukewarm water

Glaze

- ½ teaspoon vanilla extract
- ¼ teaspoon salt
- 5 tablespoons butter
- 1½ cups powdered sugar
- ¼ cup cream cheese

Filling

- 1 cup brown sugar

- 2 tablespoons cinnamon
- 5 granny smith apples
- ½ cup sugar
- 6 tablespoons melted butter

Method:

1. Add yeast and 2 tablespoons sugar to warm water in a small dish and let allowed to stand for 10 minutes, or until it combines.
2. Put the sugar, milk, egg, melted butter, and salt in a mixing bowl and beat on low speed until incorporated.
3. Mix in half of the flour until homogeneous.
4. Keep mixing at low speed after adding the yeast mixture.
5. Add the rest flour in a slow, steady stream. Increase the speed high in a stand mixer and mix for five minutes.
6. In a large pan over medium heat, melt four tablespoons of butter and all of the granulated sugar, then add the fruit.
7. Sauté until the apple releases juice, then increase the heat to moderate and cook until the fruits are slightly caramelized.
8. Combine the brown sugar and cinnamon in a bowl and sprinkle evenly over the butter.
9. Over the brown sugar, pour the apple combination.
10. Preheat the oven to 375°F as the rolls rise and bake for 20-22 minutes.

4.12 French Donuts

Crullers, which originated in the Dutch, are now popular in both the United States and Canada! French Crullers, unlike traditional donuts, are prepared using pâte à choux dough rather than yeasted dough. French Crullers are light and delicate in flavor, not heavy or greasy like ordinary doughnuts, and are ideal for weekend breakfasts.

Cooking Time: 55 minutes

Serving Size: 18 crullers

Ingredients:

- Vegetable oil (for frying)
- Vanilla doughnut glaze
- 4 large eggs, room temperature
- Zest from 1 lemon
- ½ cup whole milk
- 1 teaspoon salt
- 1 cup all-purpose flour
- ½ cup butter
- 1 tablespoon granulated sugar
- ½ cup water

Method:

1. Put the water, butter, sugar, milk, and salt to a boil in a big, heavy-bottomed pot.
2. Beat in the two additional eggs until well combined.
3. Refrigerate the dough in a sealed jar for at least one hour or until completely cold.
4. Pour 1 inch of oil into a big, heavy-bottomed pot, attach a thermometer to the pot's top, and boil to 350°F (180°C).

5. Place a sheet pan on a baking sheet and a dish of vanilla doughnut icing beside the shelf.
6. Cook crullers for 2-3 minutes on one half until lightly browned, then turn and fry for another 2-3 minutes on either side.
7. Take from the heat, dip in the sauce, and drain on a cutting board to cool.

4.13 Parmesan Garlic Bread

This fast and simple recipe transforms ordinary French bread into wonderful buttery cheese garlic bread. It is simple and quick to prepare. Simply go to the bakery area of the store and get French bread the next time you go shopping. You will have delicious garlic bread on your dinner table in no time!

Cooking Time: 25 minutes

Serving Size: 3

Ingredients:

- 5 tablespoons Parmesan cheese
- 1 teaspoon parsley leaves
- 1 ¼ stick salted butter
- 5 cloves garlic
- 1 loaf crusty French bread

Method:

1. Preheat oven to 375 degrees Fahrenheit.
2. Mix the Parmesan cheese, garlic, softened butter, and parsley in a shallow saucepan. Stir everything together well.
3. Brush a generous amount of the liquid on the divided French bread.
4. Bake for 15 minutes, or until the clove Parmesan combination has a crusty appearance.

5. Remove from the fire, let cool slightly before slicing into pieces with a bread knife. It is better to eat it when it is still warm.

4.14 Chocolate Chip Brioche

It is a delicious morning treat or dessert made with a rich, buttered cinnamon swirl with chocolate chips! Although Chocolate Chip Brioche is a quick dish, it is a fun one to prepare with kids.

Cooking Time: 20 minutes

Serving Size: 9 bars

Ingredients:
- Three handfuls of vanilla wafers
- 1 stick of melted butter
- ½ teaspoon vanilla extract
- 8 oz whipped cream
- 3.4 oz box of pudding mix
- ½ teaspoon cinnamon
- 1 cup heavy whipping cream
- 14 oz can condense milk
- 4 bananas

Method:
1. To create the crust, finely crush approximately three handfuls of caramel wafers and combine them with the butter.
2. Set it aside after pressing it into your dish.
3. Combine the pudding mix, condensed milk, whipping cream, and mashed bananas in a large mixing bowl.

4. Refrigerate for at least five minutes after adding the cinnamon and vanilla essence.
5. Get your crust out and cut sixteen slices of banana into it.
6. To make it appear nice, cover it with a coating of whipped cream and some additional wafers.

Chapter 5: Particular Ingredients French Bread Recipes

5.1 Rosemary Bread with Pecans and Dried Cranberries

This gourmet Cranberry Pecan Bread Maker recipe gets a boost from Rosemary. This recipe makes a delicious cheese sandwich. It is a chewy artisanal loaf with a sweet and flavorful crust.

Cooking Time: 3 hours 30 minutes

Serving Size: 1 loaf

Ingredients:

Pre-Ferment

- 1 teaspoon instant yeast
- 1 cup tap water
- 1-½ cups all-purpose

Dough

- ½ cup pecans
- ¾ cup dried cranberries
- 1-¾ cups all-purpose flour
- 2 teaspoons fresh rosemary
- Pre-ferment mixture
- 1 teaspoon sugar
- 1-½ teaspoon salt
- 3 tablespoons tap water

Method:

1. In the bread maker pan, combine the first three items and choose the "dough" cycle.
2. Let 5 minutes for mixing, gently pushing flour in the edges with a tiny spatula.
3. Disconnect the device and let it be at ambient temperature for 8 hours or overnight. Do not leave for more than 16 hours.
4. To the pre-ferment, add more water, sugar, salt, and flour.
5. Restart the dough-making process.
6. After 10-fifteen minutes of mixing, check the dough.
7. Add rosemary, cherries, and pecans when the machine whistles.
8. Take the dough from the bread maker pan and place it on a lightly floured surface or a baking pans mat.
9. Preheat the oven to 425 degrees about fifteen minutes before the loaf is ready to bake.
10. Bake for 30-40 minutes, or until lightly golden and internal temperature rises 190 degrees F.
11. Before cutting, let the loaf cool on a shelf.

5.2 Mushroom Bread

This yeast bread's substantial texture, rustic look, and savory taste make it a repeat hit with guests. Nothing compares to the sweet fragrance as it bakes.

Cooking Time: 55 minutes

Serving Size: 16 slices

Ingredients:

- 1 teaspoon salt
- 5-¼ cups all-purpose flour
- 2 tablespoons plain yogurt
- 2 tablespoons honey
- 2 packages of active dry yeast
- 1 cup warm water
- ¼ cup butter
- 1 medium onion
- 3 tablespoons soy sauce
- 1-pound fresh mushrooms

Method:

1. Melt the butter in a medium bowl. Sauté the mushrooms and onions until they are soft.
2. Cook and stir for another 2 minutes after adding the soy sauce. Bring to room temperature before serving.
3. Put yeast in hot water in a large mixing dish.
4. Combine the mushroom combination, salt, honey, yogurt, and 2-½ cups flour in a large mixing bowl. Blend until completely smooth.
5. Turn out onto a floured board and knead for 6-8 minutes, or until smooth and flexible.

6. Divide the dough in half and form loaves.
7. Place in two buttered 9x5-inch loaf pans.
8. Allow 45 minutes for the dough to double in size.
9. Preheat oven to 400°F and bake for 20-30 minutes, or until lightly browned.

5.3 Black Pepper Focaccia Bread

The taste of smoked paprika focaccia is not overpowering. However, it still has a great flavor, fluffy texture, and crunchy crust, making it ideal for eating alone or creating amazing sandwiches.

Cooking Time: 3 hours 20 minutes

Serving Size: 1 focaccia

Ingredients:

- Coarse sea salt, for garnish
- 1 teaspoon black pepper
- 1 ⅔ cups water
- 4 ⅛ cups bread flour
- 2 teaspoons salt
- 3 tablespoons olive oil
- 3 teaspoons yeast

Method:

1. In the mixing bowl equipped with the dough hook, pour the flour.
2. On separate ends of the dish, add a little salt and yeast, mixing each in with your fingertips.
3. Stir in the canola oil and black pepper until everything is well combined.
4. Stir half of the water into the egg mixture with the hook attachment on low speed till a stiff, oily dough forms.
5. Add additional water a little at a time until you have a sticky dough.

6. When the mixture has at least tripled in size, place it in the buttered springform pan and push it down with your fingers to the pan's sides.

7. Preheat the oven to 425°F about 30 minutes before the loaf has finished rising.

8. When the focaccia has grown enough, season it with fine kosher salt and bake it for 25 minutes at 425°F.

5.4 Kalamata Olives Bread

The salty kalamata olives in this quick artisan olive bread recipe give this rustic bread dish depth of flavor! It is a simple recipe that's sure to become a staple in your meals.

Cooking Time: 3 hours

Serving Size: 1 loaf

Ingredients:

- 2 teaspoons olive oil
- ½ cup Kalamata olives
- ½ teaspoon salt
- ½ teaspoon garlic powder
- 2 ¾ cup all-purpose flour
- 1 cup lukewarm water
- 1 ½ teaspoon instant yeast

Method:

1. In the mixing bowl, add the ingredients except for olives.
2. Allow for a 15-minute rest period to reactivate the yeast.
3. Combine the olives and fold them in.
4. Knead for five minutes on medium with the dough hook on.
5. Place the kneaded mixture in an oiled dish, cover, and let rise in a hot place for 60 minutes.
6. Preheat the oven to 400°F and put a second sheet pan on the tray.
7. Close the oven door after pouring a half cup of water over the heated baking sheet on the bottom rack.
8. Preheat oven to 350°F and bake for thirty minutes.
9. Allow cooling fully before putting it on a wire rack.

5.5 Dill Pickle Rye Bread

Tasty yeast bread with a strong dill pickle taste. This bread is the ideal accompaniment to any summer dinner or picnic. Served with hot dogs or hamburgers, this dish is fantastic.

Cooking Time: 25 minutes

Serving Size: 1 loaf

   Ingredients:
   - 1 large dill pickle
   - 1 tablespoon dill weed
   - 3 cups bread flour
   - ¼ teaspoon salt
   - 3 teaspoons instant dry yeast
   - 1 cup dill pickle juice
   - 1 tablespoon extra-virgin olive oil
   - 1 tablespoon sugar

Method:
1. Add yeast and 1 teaspoon sugar over ¼ cup pickle juice.
2. Allow settling for 10 to 15 minutes or until foamy.
3. Pour the mixture into a mixing bowl.
4. Mix the sugars, remaining pickle juice, yeast mixture, flour, oil, and salts in a mixer equipped with a flat hook attachment.
5. While beating at low speed, gradually add the remaining flour, ¼ cup at a time. Knead on the moderate speed with a dough hook.
6. Add the dill weed and sliced dill pickle.

7. Form the loaf into a circular shape and set it aside to rise in an oiled Dutch oven with a lid. Allow rising for another thirty minutes.
8. Preheat the oven to 450 degrees in the meantime.
9. Place in the oven and bake for twenty minutes.
10. Allow cooling for thirty minutes before cutting.

5.6 Quinoa Oatmeal Bread

Bring this quinoa oat to toast to your bread maker recipe list. Quinoa, oats, wheat, bread flours, buttermilk, and honey combine to make a tasty, nutritious bread with a nutty taste and chewy structure.

Cooking Time: 3 hours 50 minutes

Serving Size: 8 servings

Ingredients:

- 1½ teaspoons yeast
- 1 teaspoon salt
- 1 tablespoon sugar
- 1 tablespoon honey
- ½ cup quick-cooking oats
- 5 tablespoons butter
- 1/3 cup quinoa
- 1½ cups bread flour
- ½ cup whole wheat flour
- 1 cup buttermilk
- 2/3 cup water

Method:

1. Fill a pot halfway with water and add the rice.
2. Bring to a boil, then reduce to low heat and simmer for five minutes, covered.
3. Turn the heat down and cover the quinoa for 10 to 15 minutes.

4. Check the dough machine's instructions to see what order to put the components in.

5. In the bread maker, combine the whole wheat flour, bread flour, buttermilk, yeast, honey, oats, butter, salt, sugar, and the cooked quinoa.

6. Allow the bread maker to cycle and bake a whole grain loaf after programming it.

7. Allow at least fifteen minutes for the bread to cool before cutting.

5.7 Banana Chocolate Chip Bread

Not only is this recipe for easy-baked banana bread, but it is also the finest piece to have with your coffee in the morning!

Cooking Time: 1 hour 5 minutes

Serving Size: 14 slices

Ingredients:

- 2 teaspoons pure vanilla extract
- 1 cup chocolate chips
- 2 large eggs
- ½ cup butter melted
- 1 teaspoon cinnamon
- 3 medium ripe bananas
- 1¾ cups all-purpose flour
- 1 teaspoon baking soda
- ½ teaspoon salt
- ¼ cup brown sugar
- ¾ cup granulated white sugar

Method:

1. Preheat the oven to 350 degrees Fahrenheit.
2. Combine the flour, salt, baking soda, sugars, and cinnamon in a large mixing bowl.
3. Smash the bananas well in a different pan.
4. Then add melting butter, eggs, and vanilla extract.
5. Lightly mix the milk mixture into the dry ones using a spoon or fork until barely blended.

6. Cut it in half of the chocolate carefully.
7. Heat for 55-60 minutes, till a wooden skewer in the middle, comes out clean.

5.8 Cinnamon Raisin Bread

It is delicious, and the dough comes together wonderfully. The recipe requires the least amount of work and time to prepare.

Cooking Time: 3 hours 45 minutes

Serving Size: 3 loaves

Ingredients:

- 3 tablespoons ground cinnamon
- 2 tablespoons butter
- 2 tablespoons milk
- 1 cup white sugar
- 1 cup raisins
- 8 cups all-purpose flour
- 1 ½ cups milk
- 1 teaspoon salt
- ½ cup unsalted butter
- 3 eggs
- ½ cup white sugar
- 2 (¼ ounce) active dry yeast
- 1 cup warm water

Method:

1. Put yeast in hot water and set aside for 10 minutes, or until foamy.
2. After that, combine the sugar, eggs, salt, butter, and raisins in a mixing bowl.
3. To create a firm mixture, slowly add the flour.

4. Knead the dough for several minutes on a lightly oiled board until smooth.

5. Using your hands, wet the dough with two tablespoons of milk and spread it all over.

6. Sprinkle sugar and cinnamon evenly on top of the wet dough.

7. Bake for 30 minutes at 350 degrees, or until the loaves are golden brown and flat when pressed.

8. Remove from the oven and cool on a rack.

5.9 Sweet French Bread

This bread is the pinnacle of sweet deliciousness, and it vanishes from the table in a flash. Make a topping out of anything you like.

Cooking Time: 2 hours

Serving Size: 1 1½ pound loaves

Ingredients:

- 1½ teaspoons instant yeast
- 3¼ cups water
- 4½ cups all-purpose flour
- 1 tablespoon salt
- 4½ cups bread flour

Method:

1. In a mixing bowl, combine all items except the polenta until the dough can be shaped into a ball.
2. Dust the counter with flour, turn out the mixture, and knead it for 10-15 minutes.
3. Divide the dough into two pieces using a sharp knife.
4. Roll each ball of bread into a long rectangle to create loaves or baguettes.
5. Put the loaves in a 450°F oven after spraying them with ice water.
6. Spray them one again after 2 minutes.
7. Examine the loaves around 10 minutes after the final spray.
8. Take off the heat and place the loaves in a warm oven for another 10 minutes if they look golden and done.

5.10 Chocolate Bread Recipe

Try this simple Chocolate Bread recipe. A delectable handmade cake that's fast, simple, and a chocoholic! This simple and low-cost dish is fast and easy to make yet tastes delicious.

Cooking Time: 1 hour 15 minutes

Serving Size: 1 loaf

Ingredients:

- 180 ml buttermilk
- 110 grams chocolate chips
- 1 teaspoon vanilla extract
- 2 large eggs
- 175 grams plain flour
- 50 grams caster sugar
- 115 grams butter
- 1½ teaspoons baking powder
- 90 grams brown sugar
- 1 teaspoon baking soda
- 40 grams cocoa powder

Method:

1. Preheat the oven to 180 degrees Celsius.
2. Mix baking soda, cocoa, flour, and baking powder in a large mixing dish. Stir in the sugars gradually.
3. In a large heatproof dish, melt the butter in the microwaves in 20 seconds bursts, whisking in between.
4. In a small bowl, mix the vanilla and eggs until well blended.

5. Create a well in the center of the flour mixture, then pour in the wet ingredients and buttermilk.
6. Add 75-gram (½ cup) chocolate chips to the batter.
7. Preheat oven to 350°F and bake for 45 minutes, or until a knife inserted in the middle comes out clean. Place on a wire rack to cool fully.

5.11 Sweetened Condensed Milk White Bread

This simple bread recipe uses readily accessible materials to create a piece of bread with hot milk.

Cooking Time: 2 hours 45 minutes

Serving Size: 8-10

> **Ingredients:**
> - 1 teaspoon salt
> - 3½ cups bread flour
> - ½ cup sweetened condensed milk
> - 1 tablespoon butter
> - 2 teaspoons active dry yeast
> - 1 cup water

Method:
1. Combine water and yeast in a small mixing dish.
2. Combine the condensed milk, oil, and salt in a mixing bowl.
3. Slowly incorporate the leftover flour, just enough to form a dough that leads the spoon around the dish.
4. Make a loaf out of the dough.
5. Preheat oven to 350°F and bake loaf for 45 minutes, or until lightly browned.
6. Remove the loaf from the baking pan and place it on a cooling rack to cool.

5.12 Potato Dinner Rolls with Honey Glaze

These Sweet Potato Balls are made in the Bread Maker using the Loaf cycle, then cooked in the oven. The glaze is delicious and sweet.

Cooking Time: 3 hours

Serving Size: 16 rolls

Ingredients:

Dough

- 3 cups bread flour
- 2 teaspoons instant yeast
- 2/3 cup warm milk
- Dash of cinnamon
- 1 teaspoon salt
- ¼ cup butter
- 1 egg
- ¼ cup sugar
- ½ cup mashed sweet potato

Honey Butter Glaze

- 1 tablespoon butter
- 3 tablespoons sugar
- 2 tablespoons honey
- 1 egg white

Method:

1. Toss the specified ingredients into the bread maker pan.

2. Place the dough on a floured board after removing it from the bread maker.
3. Make four pieces by dividing the dough in half and then half again.
4. Divide each of these portions into four pieces of dough, resulting in 16 little dough balls.
5. Make round balls out of the dough.
6. Preheat oven to 350°F and bake rolls for 12-15 minutes, or until lightly browned.
7. Allow cooling in the pan or on a baking sheet.
8. Glaze the bread with glazing ingredients.

5.13 French Bear Claws

The soft dough, creamy almond center, and beautiful fanned topped with honey and nuts are hard to resist.

Cooking Time: 1 hour

Serving Size: 18 claws

Ingredients:

- Sugar or coarse sugar
- Sliced almonds
- ½ cup almond paste
- 1 tablespoon water
- 1-½ cups cold butter
- 1 large egg white
- ¾ cup confectioners' sugar
- ¼ teaspoon salt
- 2 large eggs
- 5 cups all-purpose flour
- 1-¼ cups half-and-half cream
- ¼ cup sugar
- 1 package active dry yeast

Method:

1. Toss 3 cups flour with oil in a mixing dish until thoroughly combined; set aside.
2. Combine the yeast and the additional flour in a large mixing pan.
3. Heat the sugar, cream, and salt in a pot.

4. Add 1 egg to the yeast mixture. Blend until completely smooth.
5. Stir in the butter mixture until smooth.
6. Add confectioners' sugar and almonds paste slowly, beating until smooth.
7. Using a knife, cut the dough in half widthwise.
8. Fill each with approximately 2 teaspoons of the filling.
9. Fold the long sides over the filling and secure the edges and ends. Cut each piece into three parts.
10. Brush dough with a little mixture of water and the leftover egg.
11. Preheat oven to 375°F and bake for fifteen minutes, or until lightly golden. Cool on wire racks after removing from pans.

5.14 Golden Egg Bread with Dried Fruit

This is a light-textured bread maker recipe that's great for French toast and hot dogs. It is easy to make and fruity flavor recipe.

Cooking Time: 3 hours 15 minutes

Serving Size: 1 loaf

Ingredients:

- 3 cups bread flour
- 2 teaspoons instant yeast
- 1½ teaspoons table salt
- 2/3 cup dried cranberries
- ¾ cup water
- 6 tablespoons vegetable oil
- ¼ cup granulated sugar
- 2 large eggs

Method:

1. In the bread maker pan, layer the items in the sequence listed.
2. If required, add 1 tablespoon of flour at a time until the dough is thick enough to form a ball and barely clear the sides.
3. Start the dough cycle on the machine.
4. When the dough is finished, it should have doubled in size. If not, leave it in the machine to rise.
5. Preheat the oven to 350 degrees Fahrenheit.
6. Bake for 45 minutes, or until the chicken is cooked through and the crust is pale yellow.
7. Allow thirty seconds on the counter before withdrawing from the pan.

Chapter 6: Diet French Bread Recipes

6.1 Keto Bread

This soft, simple white keto bread contains just five components and 1 net carb per serving.

Cooking Time: 1 hour 20 minutes

Serving Size: 18 servings

> **Ingredients:**
> - 1/3 cup butter
> - 12 large egg whites
> - 2 teaspoon baking powder
> - ¼ teaspoon sea salt
> - ¼ cup coconut flour
> - 1 cup almond flour

Method:
1. Preheat the oven to 350 degrees Fahrenheit.
2. Mix the baking powder, coconut flour, almond flour, xanthan gum, erythritol, and sea salt in a large mixing bowl.
3. Pulse until everything is well mixed.
4. Pour the softened butter into the pan.
5. Using a hand mixer, whip the egg yolks and cream of tartar until firm peaks form in a very large mixing basin.
6. Add ½ of the egg whites to the food processor.
7. Pulse a few times until everything is well mixed.
8. Transfer the mixture from the stick blender to the mixing bowl with the egg yolks, and carefully fold until there are no streaks left.

9. Smooth the top of the batter into the prepared loaf pan.
10. Bake for approximately 40 minutes, or until lightly browned on top.

6.2 No-Milk Bread Recipe

Most homemade bread recipes call for dairy, making it difficult to locate a good recipe if you are allergic or do not eat milk products. Or maybe you have just run out of milk. Whatever your problem, this simple braided wheat bread recipe is here to help.

Cooking Time: 2 hours 45 minutes

Serving Size: 10

Ingredients:

- 1 teaspoon kosher salt
- 3 cups bread flour
- 1½ tablespoons granulated sugar
- 1 tablespoon vegetable oil
- 2½ teaspoons active dry yeast
- 1¼ cups water

Method:

1. Combine the water and yeast in a small mixing pan.
2. Stir in the oil, sugar, and salt.
3. Mix in 2 cups of wheat flour well.
4. Add the rest flour at a slow speed.
5. Knead the dough for four minutes on a well-floured work surface.
6. Make three equal portions of the dough.
7. Braid the dough pieces together at the bottom and squeeze the ends together.
8. Preheat the oven to 350°F and bake the loaf for 35–40 minutes, or until golden brown.

6.3 Low Carb Yeast Bread

Aside from the items you use and the method you follow, the form and size of your bread loaf may impact the outcome. This easy low-yeast recipe is all you need to try for a perfect breakfast.

Cooking Time: 2 hours 30 minutes

Serving Size: 1 loaf

> **Ingredients:**
>
> **Wet Ingredients**
>
> - 3 large egg yolks
> - 2 tablespoon apple cider vinegar
> - 1 tablespoon yacon syrup
> - 5 large egg whites
> - 2 cups warm water
>
> **Dry Ingredients**
>
> - ½ teaspoon baking soda
> - 1 teaspoon sea salt
> - 6 tablespoon psyllium husks
> - 1 teaspoon cream of tartar
> - ½ cup coconut flour
> - ¼ cup whey protein powder
> - 1¼ cup sesame seed flour
> - ½ cup packed flax meal
> - 1 tablespoon active dry yeast

Method:

1. In a dish, pour ¾ cup of water.
2. Stir in the yacon syrup or sugars until it is completely dissolved.
3. Sprinkle active dry yeast on top.
4. Preheat the oven to 350°F. Place the dish in the oven. Wait 10 minutes for proofing.
5. In the meanwhile, crush the entire psyllium husks in a stick blender until powdered.
6. In a mixing basin, combine the other dry ingredients.
7. To process well, mix to incorporate or use a hand mixer.
8. In a mixing dish, combine all of the egg yolks and two egg whites.
9. In the dish containing the proofed yeast, combine the egg whites and yolks. Combine the vinegar and the leftover warm water in a mixing bowl.
10. Process thoroughly as you add the dry ingredients, approximately ½ cup at a time.
11. Place the dough in the loaf pan that has been prepared.
12. Preheat oven to 350°F and bake for 60 minutes.

6.4 Fat-Free Wheat Bread

This bread is simple to prepare and tasty. Add the items in the sequence recommended in your machine's handbook for optimum results.

Cooking Time: 2 hours 35 minutes

Serving Size: 12

Ingredients:

- 1½ teaspoon salt
- 2½ teaspoon rapid rise yeast
- Four tablespoons wheat gluten
- 2 tablespoons sugar
- 4 2/3 cups whole wheat flour
- 1 cup chickpea broth

Method:

1. In the bread machine's pan, pour in the water or chickpeas stock.
2. In the order indicated, add the rest of the ingredients.
3. A quick-bake whole wheat cycle or a normal whole wheat cycle are also options. Start by pressing the start button.
4. When the bread is done baking, remove it from the oven.
5. Allowing the bread to cool before slicing it improves the quality of the slices.

6.5 Whole-Wheat Bread

Wheat bread is unquestionably a healthier option since whole wheat flour contains much more fiber and nutrients than highly processed white flour.

Cooking Time: 1 hour

Serving Size: 12 slices

Ingredients:

- 3 ¾ cups whole wheat flour
- ½ teaspoon kosher salt
- ¼ cup honey
- 3 tablespoons unsalted butter
- ¼ ounce active dry yeast
- 1½ cups warm water

Method:

1. In a large mixing bowl, combine the hot water and yeast.
2. Let for a 5-minute proofing period for the yeast.
3. Combine the sugar and butter in a mixing bowl.
4. Mix in two cups of flour and the salt till the mixture is moistened.
5. For 3 minutes, beat on moderate speed.
6. Knead for 10 minutes on a baking sheet, adding ¾ cup more flour as needed until dough is thick and elastic.
7. Preheat the oven to 350 degrees Fahrenheit.
8. Uncover the dough and bake for 35 to 40 minutes, or until a flat sound is heard gently tapping the bottom.

6.6 Oatmeal Bread Recipe

This delicate, high-rising sandwiches bread is light enough for children to enjoy while being nutritious enough for various side dishes. It also makes excellent toast, which goes well with jam or buttery mashed potatoes.

Cooking Time: 2 hours 50 minutes

Serving Size: 1 loaf

Ingredients:

Dough

- 2 teaspoons instant yeast
- 1¼ cups lukewarm milk
- 1½ teaspoons salt
- 3 tablespoons brown sugar
- 1 cup old-fashioned rolled oats
- 2 tablespoons butter
- 3 cups bread flour

Topping

- 1 tablespoon cold water
- 2 tablespoons rolled oats
- 1 large egg white

Method:

1. To make a rough, shaggy dough, combine all of the items in a large mixing dish or the bowl of a stick blender.
2. Make a form using the dough on a lightly greased surface.
3. Preheat your oven to 350°F with a rack in the middle towards the end of the rising period.

4. Brush the beaten egg white all over the outer layer, then scatter the rolled oats on top.

5. Preheat the oven to 350°F and bake the bread for 35–40 minutes, or until lightly golden.

6. Remove the loaf from the pan and let it cool on a cooling rack.

6.7 Basic White Bread (no-milk)

It may seem overwhelming if you have never made bread before, but this recipe is simple to follow and always turns out perfectly!

Cooking Time: 1 hour 55 minutes

Serving Size: 16 slices

Ingredients:

- 4 cups flour
- 2 teaspoons yeast
- 2 tablespoons oil
- 1 teaspoon salt
- 4 tablespoons honey
- 1 1/3 cup water

Method:

1. Place all of the items in your bread machine in the sequence recommended by your device.
2. Select the dough cycle on your bread maker and press the start button.
3. Place the dough in two oiled loaf pans and form it into two loaves.
4. Preheat the oven to 400 degrees Fahrenheit and bake for 15 to 20 minutes, or until lightly browned.

6.8 Gluten-Free Bread

A gluten-free loaf recipe that's easy to prepare, dairy-free, and cooks up to be the finest gluten-free bread you have ever had. Make gluten-free bread for your next meal.

Cooking Time: 1 hour 15 minutes

Serving Size: 1 loaf

Ingredients:

For the Yeast Proof

- 2 tablespoons sugar
- 2¼ teaspoons dry active yeast
- 1¼ cup water

For the Bread

- 3 egg whites
- 1 teaspoon apple cider vinegar
- 1 teaspoon salt
- ¼ cup oil of choice
- 1 cup white rice flour
- 2½ teaspoons xanthan gum
- 1 teaspoon baking powder
- ¾ cup tapioca starch
- ½ cup millet flour
- ¼ cup ground flaxseed
- ¾ cup potato starch

Method:

1. Stir together the sugar and yeast in hot water; leave aside for 5-10 minutes, but no more.
2. While the yeast is proving, combine the flaxseed meal, flours, baking powder, xanthan gum, and salt in the mixing bowl equipped with the dough hook.
3. Reduce the speed of your mixer to medium and beat just until everything is incorporated.
4. Add the egg whites, oil, vinegar, and proofed yeast mixture to the mixer while still running.
5. Increase the mixer's speed to low and mix for another 2 - 3 minutes.
6. Preheat the oven to 350 degrees Fahrenheit. Bake for 55–60 minutes after removing the plastic wrap.

6.9 Vegan Bread

With just three ingredients: water, wheat, and quick yeast, this crusty handmade and extremely simple vegan bread recipe come together quickly. Plant-based, no kneading required, no special equipment required, and no oil is used.

Cooking Time: 40 minutes

Serving Size: 8

Ingredients:

- 2 teaspoon instant dry yeast
- 1 teaspoon sea salt
- 1.5 cups warm water
- 3.25 cups all-purpose flour

Method:

1. Combine the all-purpose flour, yeast, and sea salt in a food processor or blender or your kitchen aid mixer.
2. Stir in the water until it is completely mixed.
3. Fold it in upon itself a few times and make it form a circular loaf.
4. Meantime, preheat your oven to 450 degrees Fahrenheit and place a pizza stone inside.
5. Put a little semolina flour on the sheet pan, then carefully slide the pizza dough onto it.
6. Cook until lightly browned, approximately 30 minutes.

6.10 Keto Sandwich Bread

That's the one if you are searching for a new gluten-free and ketogenic sandwiches bread recipe. It has a light and delicate texture, a little crust, and is not eggy or crumbly!

Cooking Time: 1 hour 35 minutes

Serving Size: 14 slices

Ingredients:

- 8 large egg whites
- ¼ teaspoon cream of tartar
- 1 tablespoon keto sweetener
- ¼ cup melted butter
- 2 teaspoon baking powder
- ½ teaspoon xanthan gum
- 2 cups almond flour
- ¾ teaspoon sea salt
- ¼ cup ground flax seeds

Method:

1. Preheat the oven to 350°F.
2. Lightly coat an 8x4-inch loaf pan with avocados or olive oil.
3. Whisk together all the ground flax seeds, toasted almond flour, sea salt, xanthan gum, baking powder, and honey in a large mixing dish.
4. Melt the butter, then mix it into the flour mixture using a fork or a whisk.
5. Whisk the egg yolks and cream of tartar in a large serving dish.
6. Add half of the eggs and beat completely.

7. Then, carefully mix the batter into the bowl with the leftover egg yolks until no streaks remain.
8. Bake for 40 - 50 minutes, or until lightly browned on top. Then bake for another 25 to 30 minutes, tenting the top with aluminum foil.

6.11 Bread Maker Feta and Olive Crusty Low Carb Bread

Olives may be cut coarsely or finely, depending on personal preference. For a delicious alternative, use any hard cheese and herbs of your choosing.

Cooking Time: 3 hours 28 minutes

Serving Size: 14 slices

Ingredients:

- Pinch salt flakes
- ½ teaspoon xanthan gum
- ½ cup gentle fiber
- 1¼ cup gluten flour
- 60 g butter cubed
- 2/3 cup chia flour
- 1 cup warm water
- 1 tablespoon yeast
- 1 egg lightly whisked
- 1 tablespoon honey

Method:

1. Take the bread pan out of the bread machine.
2. In a small dish, whisk together honey, warm water, and yeast until frothy.
3. Place the additional bread ingredients in the order shown in the ingredients list into the bread pan and return to the bread maker.
4. Start by selecting menu three and white-filled bread.

5. A buzzing sound will be heard after approximately 20-25 minutes.
6. Cover the lid on the pan and add the kalamata olives, feta, and cilantro. To proceed, press start.
7. When the bread machine beeps again, it is time to take your bread and switch it off.

6.12 Sugar-Free Bread

This is a 5-ingredient, low-cost whole wheat bread method that requires very little hands-on time and no essential items. It is soft, thick, crusty, and delicious!

Cooking Time: 2 hours 30 minutes

Serving Size: 12 slices

Ingredients:

- 3 tablespoons olive oil
- 1/3 cup tepid water
- 1 tablespoon instant yeast
- 2 teaspoons salt
- 200g whole-wheat flour
- 300g all-purpose white flour

Method:

1. In the mixing bowl, combine yeast, both flours, and salt.
2. Combine the olive oil and water in a mixing bowl.
3. Make the dough for ten minutes using the stand mixer.
4. Knead the dough for five to ten minutes, or until it is smooth.
5. Put the dough onto a dry, lightly floured work surface and form it after it doubled in size.
6. Preheat the oven to 400 degrees Fahrenheit and bake for thirty minutes.

6.13 Gluten-Free Pizza Dough Recipe

One of the essential things to have in your home is a simple gluten-free pizza dough mix. It is easy to prepare, freezes nicely, and melts quickly.

Cooking Time: 15 minutes

Serving Size: 2, 12- inch

Ingredients:

- 1 1/8 cup warm water
- ¼ cup extra-virgin olive oil
- 1 ½ teaspoons sugar
- 1 ½ teaspoon kosher salt
- 2 ¼ teaspoons xanthan gum
- 1 tablespoon instant yeast
- 3 cups all-purpose flour

Method:

1. Put the yeast, flour, xanthan gum, and sugar in the pan of your bread maker and stir to incorporate using a separate, manual mix.
2. Whisk in the salt until everything is thoroughly combined.
3. Combine the water and olive oil in a mixing bowl.
4. Place the dough in a greased container.
5. Place the dough in a warm environment or refrigerate for up to three days.
6. Preheat the oven to 400°F and put a pizza stone or inverted rimmed sheet pan in it when you are ready to make the pizzas.

7. Put in an oven and bake for approximately five minutes, or until the bottom of the crust has started to crisp.

Conclusion

Baking bread is both challenging and rewarding. However, since there are so many resources accessible today, the baking procedure will be extremely simple. Many people, however, are concerned about using a bread machine for baking their bread. Baking bread without a bread machine is also an easy task to do. Bread baking in the oven needs regulating the oven temperature and allowing the bread enough time to bake. Freshly baked bread is the most delicious thing that a person can eat early in the morning. The only issue is that work and focus are needed. Many people have never made bread before, but with the instructions of this book, anyone can be a professional bread baker. You can turn your kitchens into the bakery and eat your own freshly baked bread every day at a lower price than you would pay in a store. It is simple to take organic ingredients and turns them into a lovely loaf of bread. With the proper beginner's bread recipe, you should be able to succeed on the first try. Whether your first effort is successful or not, keep practicing, and your bakes will improve. Start reading this bread book and prepare fresh and tasty bread at home with these quick recipes.

www.ingramcontent.com/pod-product-compliance
Lightning Source LLC
Chambersburg PA
CBHW071502070526
44578CB00001B/417